Sanskrit is Fun

PART III

A Sanskrit Coursebook for Beginners

BOOK III

Edited by
WARWICK & ELENA JESSUP

MOTILAL BANARSIDASS
PUBLISHING HOUSE • DELHI
Email: mlbd@mlbd.in • Website: www.mlbd.in

2nd Revised Edition : Delhi ***2020***
First Indian Edition : Delhi, 2012
First Edition : London, 2005

Published by arrangement with
The Independent Educational Association Ltd
St James Schools
Sanskrit Department, London
https://www.stjamesschools.co.uk

ISBN: 978-93-90064-23-6 (PB Part I)
ISBN: 978-93-90064-24-3 (PB Part II)
ISBN: 978-93-90064-25-0 (PB Part III)
ISBN: 978-93-90064-51-9 (Set)

The Sanskritpada™, SComp™ and Flags2 Sanskrit fonts used in this book are designed and distributed by David Hockley (tel. +44 7711 794 495). © 2003 David Hockley.

COVER DRAWING: Parrot with Sanskrit lettering

Printed & Published by
Motilal Banarsidass Publishing House
A-44, Naraina Industrial Area, Phase I,
New Delhi–110 028 (INDIA)
Email: mlbd@mlbd.in
Website: www.mlbd.in

Foreword

by Prof Dr Satya Vrat Shastri

After a thorough perusal of these text books written by teachers of St James Schools in London for the teaching of Sanskrit, I am convinced of their utility for Indian schools. They are well-graded and supported by appropriate illustrations that make them very attractive to learners, particularly the young.

Today many Indian universities offer Sanskrit as an optional subject, even for those who are majoring in other subjects. For these students the books would be very effective in introducing them to Sanskrit which they might not have studied previously. The books could also be useful for those involved in performing arts like dance and music, or for students of Yoga and Ayurveda, subjects which have many Sanskrit references.

The first group of books entitled Sanskrit is Fun (3 volumes) introduce the learners to the Devanagari alphabet grouping the letters according to their place of articulation. Each group is given a designation, 'Family'. The 'Family' comprises both the vowels and the consonants. The learners are first taught how to draw the letters. The teaching is also helped by the humorous presentation of them in the form of animal figures. The next step is to add vowels to the consonants and then to teach joint consonants. Finally words and sentences are formed.

The second group of books seek to teach Sanskrit with reference to age-old stories of Krishna (2 volumes) and Rama (2 volumes). These stories with perennial interest of their own are then pressed into service to teach vocabulary, the formation of nouns and the conjugation of verbs in all three tenses. Adjectives and prepositions are also covered .

By the time learners have completed these books it is expected they would have a good basic grasp of the Sanskrit language, its vocabulary, structure and grammar. These books are an attempt to teach Sanskrit in a simple and systematic way that may well dispel the notion that Sanskrit is a difficult language.

Dr Shastri is currently an Honorary Professor at the Special Centre for Sanskrit Studies, Jawaharlal Nehru University, New Delhi. He was the Head of the Department of Sanskrit and the Dean of the Faculty of Arts at the University of Delhi, where he was the Pandit Manmohan Nath Dar Professor of Sanskrit (1970–1995).

Preface

by Professor Richard Gombrich

It is a privilege for me to be invited to introduce this set of textbooks. They have been compiled with loving care by the teachers of the Sanskrit Department of St James School in London. Their slow birth reflects the years of teaching experience which have gone into their making.

Sanskrit is by no means an easy language: even in India it is mastered only by a small minority of the population. The grammar is complicated, even if someone who masters it will finally discover that it is more systematic and less irregular than that of English. The vocabulary is vast, reflecting the vast span of time and geographical area over which Sanskrit has been used. Learning to read and write an Indian script is also a major undertaking for a student from another culture. (Luckily for us Europeans, at least it is written left to write and top to bottom.)

On the other hand, Sanskrit is not only a beautiful language written in a beautiful script; it is the vehicle of classical Indian culture, the culture which has given the world one of its greatest literatures and greatest civilizations. Sanskrit achieved something not very different from the form it still has today more than three thousand years ago. The reason why it has survived so well, and may well outlive most of the languages which the world is now using, is not hard to understand: it is because of the aesthetic attractions and the intellectual and spiritual value of the content of so many Sanskrit texts.

Only a few students are likely to have the opportunity to go on to study Sanskrit in depth, so that they can enjoy reading Sanskrit by themselves. There will be so many rival claims on their attention. But even those who only work through these books are likely to look back on the experience with satisfaction, a feeling that they have done something truly worth while. And the few who go further will be grateful that these books have launched them on an unforgettable experience.

Prof Gombrich was the Boden Professor of Sanskrit at the University of Oxford from 1976 to 2004 and was a past President of the Pali Text Society (1994–2002) and General Editor Emeritus of the Clay Sanskrit Library. He is currently the Boden Professor of Sanskrit Emeritus, University of Oxford

Notes for Teachers and Students

Part Three: Conjunct Consonants

Ideally, the students should see the writing of the letter or conjunct demonstrated and then copy it , perhaps one part at a time, depending on how complicated it is.

In general, the order for writing each letter is as follows:

- *(a) the top line is drawn first,*
- *(b) then the descender,*
- *(c) then any additional shapes.*

When writing a letter or conjunct, the student should hear the sound in mind. Each time the student hears the sound of the letter in mind while writing it, the connection between sound and shape is reinforced.

The students should always be encouraged to write each character more perfectly than the one before. This ensures that the writing improves rather than deteriorates.

It is worth mentioning that both traditionally and in the best modern practice the top line of each letter is written first and, even when writing words, only enough of this line is written for one letter at a time.

READING PRACTICE

Daily reading charts are given at regular intervals during the course to provide the necessary practice. These should be read every day until another reading chart is given in the text. This practice is only effective if the teacher ensures that each student's finger is exactly beneath the letter or conjunct being read. When the students can read a page fluently they should be asked to read it backwards (i.e., moving from right to left).

DAILY AND WEEKLY TESTING

No written course can act as a substitute for a teacher's or student's intelligence and ingenuity. Ideally, each step would be measured precisely to the needs of each pupil. Tests need to be given to ensure that the student is ready for the next stage. The following should be practised regularly:

- *(a) reading of letters, conjuncts and words written in a random order on the blackboard (or, in the case of a student, on paper), and*

- *(b) dictation: a weekly dictation of the letters or conjuncts covered that week and in previous weeks. This stimulates the student's interest in learning and acts as a guide for the teacher as to the effectiveness of the teaching.*

THE WRITING OF SANSKRIT

Each Sanskrit letter is a 'character' and can be appreciated best in the initial stages by writing without reliance on any guidelines on the page. After a little while a top line is useful from which to hang the letters. Each letter should be hung freely from this line without attempting to touch a bottom line. In this respect, it is comparable to English writing, where the letters rest on the bottom line and there is no attempt to touch the top line. Thus, in Sanskrit, there will normally be a space between the bottom of the letters and the next line down. In the case of 'double-decker' conjuncts, this rule may occasionally be broken.

There is another factor to note in the writing of Sanskrit letters. Calligraphy has traditionally been done on a slanting surface, and this is recommended for the writing of Sanskrit. One reason for this is that the student's back is thereby allowed to be more upright and there is a closer view of the writing, encouraging finer attention.

When a consonant is added to another consonant, the writing should follow the order of the sound.

SANSKRIT RECITATION

As was noted for the previous part of this course, during the learning of any language, whilst the elements of that language are being introduced, it is helpful if examples of Sanskrit literature are recited on a daily basis. This gives a taste of the beauty of the language.

Audio and video resources are available at: www.sanskritexams.org.uk

Daily Reading Chart 10

अ आ इ ई उ ऊ ऋ ॠ ऌ

ए ओ ऐ औ

अ क ख ग घ ङ ह

इ च छ ज झ ञ य श

ऋ ट ठ ड ढ ण र ष

ऌ त थ द ध न ल स

उ प फ ब भ म व

Daily Reading Chart 11

क	च	ष	त	प
का	चा	षा	ता	पा
कि	चि	षि	ति	पि
की	ची	षी	ती	पी
कु	चु	षु	तु	पु
कू	चू	षू	तू	पू
कृ	चृ	षृ	तृ	पृ
के	चे	षे	ते	पे
को	चो	षो	तो	पो
कै	चै	षै	तै	पै
कौ	चौ	षौ	तौ	पौ

Happy Halantas

When we leave out the अ of a letter we put a halanta sign next to the letter. Read and copy the following:

क	क्
म	म्
त	त्
च	च्
स	स्
श	श्
न	न्

Reading Practice

Read the following across:

त	तम	तम्	
क	कम	कम्	
त	तत	तत्	
य	यत	यत्	
व	वा	वाच	वाच्
व	वि	विश	विश्
ऋ	ऋक	ऋक्	
य	यजु	यजुस	यजुस्

Reading and Writing Practice

Read the following words and then copy them:

तम्	
कम्	
तत्	
यत्	
वाच्	
विश्	
ऋक्	
यजुस्	

The Shark Game

What is in the shark's belly?
Here are some English words written in Sanskrit letters. Read them and write the word in English.

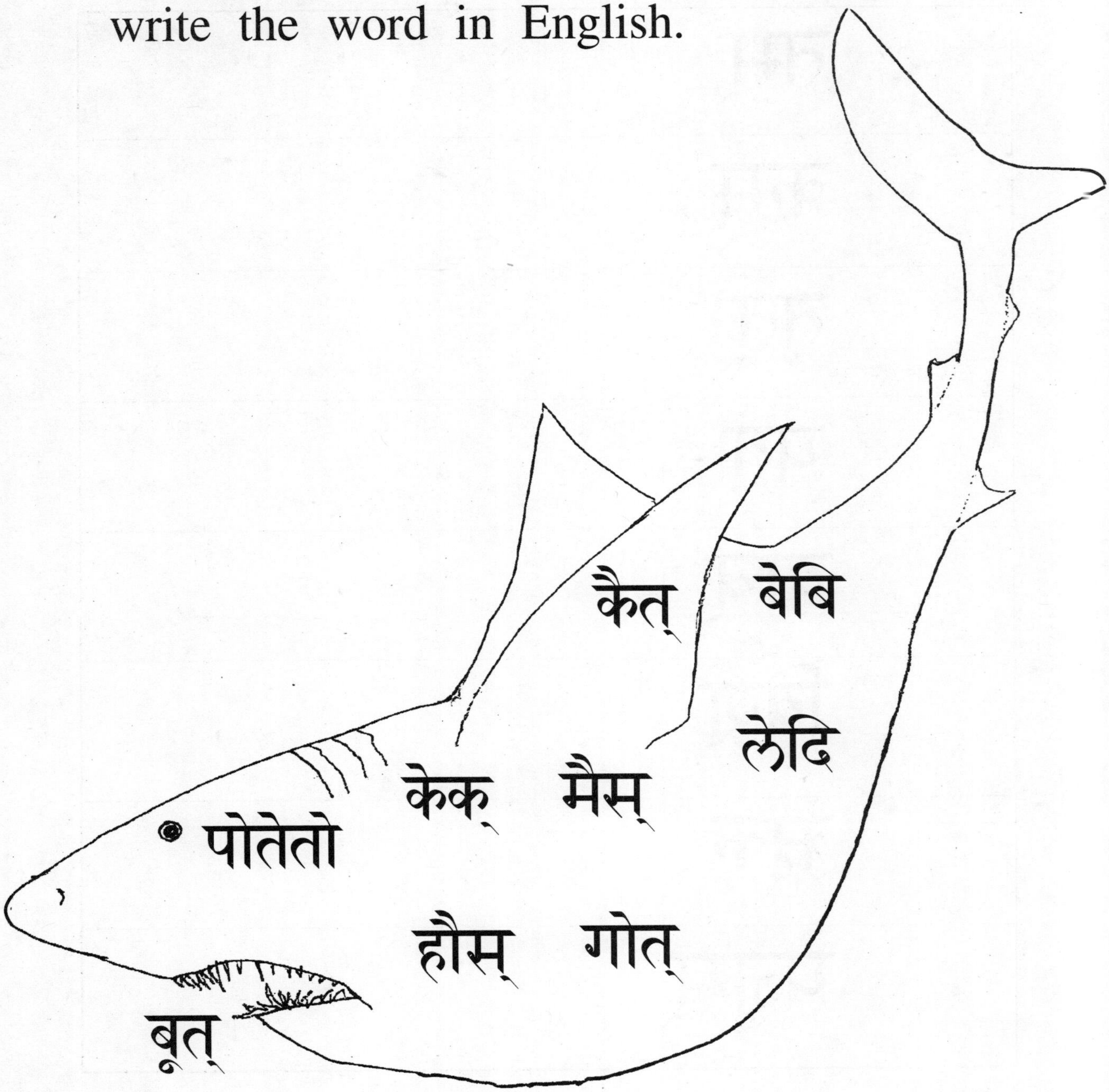

Reading Practice

Read the following across, then copy:

ज	जल	जलम्
....	....	....
फ	फल	फलम्
....	....	....
व	वन	वनम्
....	....	....
गृ	गृह	गृहम्
....	....	....
न	नगर	नगरम्
....	....	....

Link Game

Read the Sanskrit words. Now link them to their correct picture.

रेन्

बलून्

बोत्

बनान

कोत्

तै

बोन्

कौ

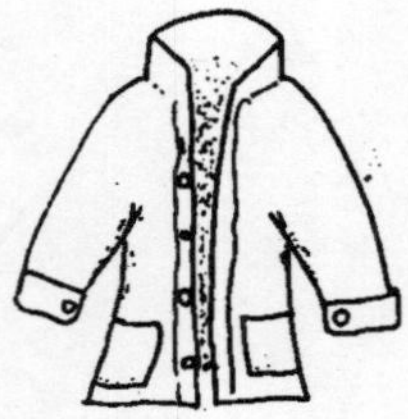

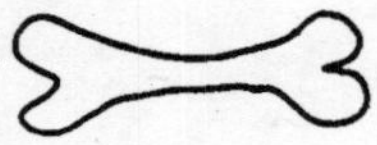

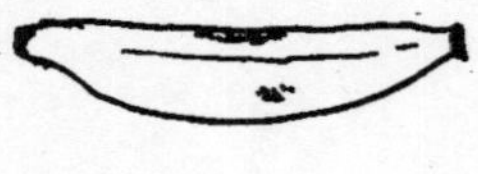

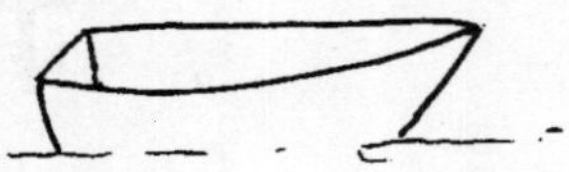

Hidden Halantas

When we leave out the अ of a letter, we put a halanta sign.
Copy and sound these letters with their halanta signs:

त् .... क् .... न् ....

So far, we have always found halanta letters at the end of words.
Read and copy these words:

हत्	....
तिप्	....
पीच्	....
गूस्	....
होम्	....

Note to Teacher/Student: A halanta is written in a different way when it is found in the middle of a word. Both the descender of the letter and the halanta sign are omitted.

Hidden Halantas

When a halanta is written in the middle of a word, it is written in the following way. Copy the second halanta letter.

प् becomes प्‍ ....

त् becomes त्‍ ....

च् becomes च्‍ ....

Take away the downward line and the halanta for these:

म् becomes ....

ष् becomes ....

स् becomes ....

न् becomes ....

ग् becomes ....

Note to Teacher/Student: The dot in the word संयोग *is called an 'anusvára' and is pronounced as a nasal sound.*

संयोग

Now we add another letter to our halanta letters. This is called a संयोग.

Read the following examples:

प्	with	ल	becomes	प्ल
त्	with	म	becomes	त्म
च्	with	छ	becomes	च्छ
म्	with	भ	becomes	म्भ
ष्	with	ण	becomes	ष्ण

Note to Teacher/Student: The + sign and the arrow symbol take the place of the words 'with' and ' becomes' respectively.

Read and copy the following examples.

प्	+	ल	→	प्ल
....	+	....	→	....

त्	+	म	→	त्म
....	+	....	→	....

च्	+	छ	→	च्छ
....	+	....	→	....

म्	+	भ	→	म्भ
....	+	....	→	....

ष्	+	ण	→	ष्ण
....	+	....	→	....

Join these संयोग.

म् + भ → ....

प् + ल → ....

च् + छ → ....

त् + म → ....

ष् + ण → ....

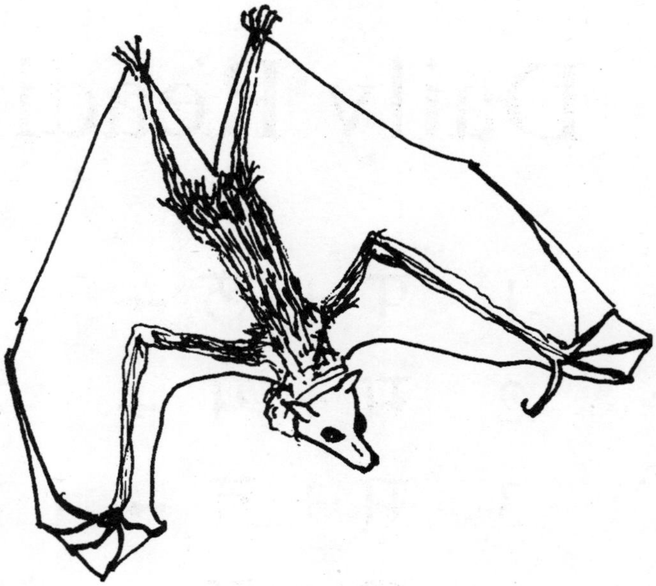

Now try these!

ष् + प → ....

व् + य → ....

स् + त → ....

स् + य → ....

श् + य → ....

श् + व → ....

न् + त → ....

✪ BONUS ✪

Now try this one!

त् + स् + य ....

Daily Reading Chart 12

1	प् + ल →	प्ल	प्लवनम्
2	स् + य →	स्य	आस्यम्
3	स् + त →	स्त	हस्तः
4	न् + त →	न्त	अनन्त
5	व् + य →	व्य	व्यापादय
6	ष् + प →	ष्प	पुष्पम्
7	ष् + ण →	ष्ण	कृष्ण
8	च् + छ →	च्छ	गच्छ
9	म् + भ →	म्भ	स्तम्भः
10	श् + व →	श्व	अश्वः
11	श् + य →	श्य	पश्यति
12	त् + म →	त्म	आत्मा
13	त् + स् + य →	त्स्य	मत्स्यः

The Millipede

Read the following संयोगs on the millipede's back:

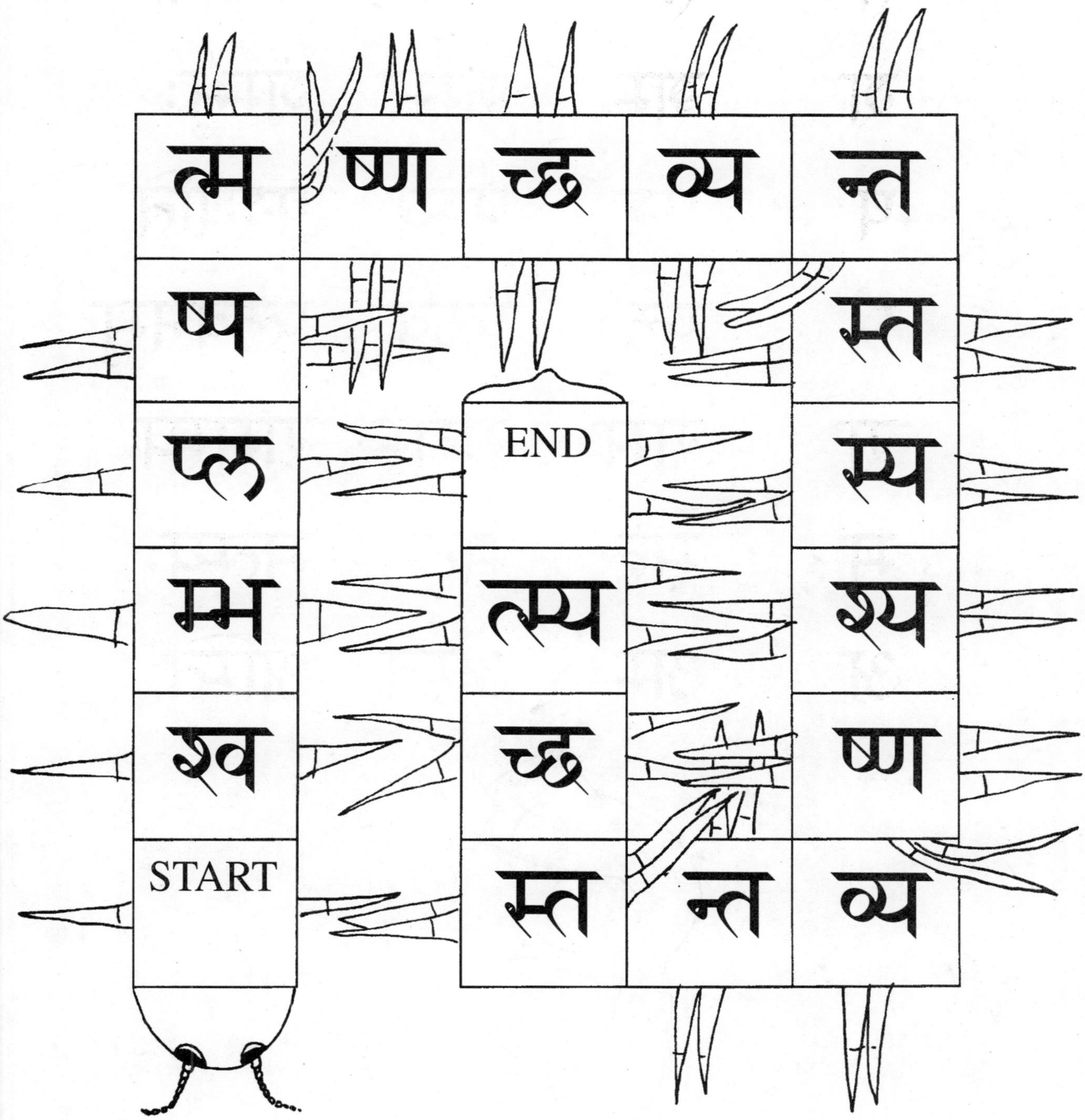

Reading Practice

Read the following across:

ह	हस्	हस्त	हस्तः
श	शम्	शम्भ	शम्भुः
प	पश्	पश्य	पश्यति
प्	प्ल	प्लव	प्लवनम्
रा	राम	रामस्	रामस्य
म	मत्	मत्स्	मत्स्यः
अ	अस्	अस्त	अस्ति

Reading Practice

Read the following and then copy:

हस्तः	....
रामस्य	....
मत्स्यः	....
पश्यति	....
प्लवनम्	....
शम्भुः	....
अस्ति	....

Reading Practice

Read the following across:

आ	आत्	आत्म	आत्मा
कृ	कृष्	कृष्ण	कृष्णः
ग	गच्	गच्छ	गच्छति
आ	आस्	आस्य	आस्यम्
पु	पुष्	पुष्प	पुष्पम्

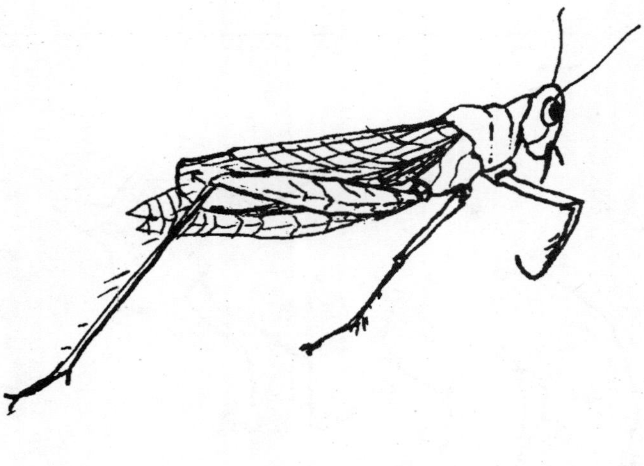

Reading Practice

Read the following and then copy:

गच्छति	....
पुष्पम्	....
आस्यम्	....
कृष्णः	....
आत्मा	....

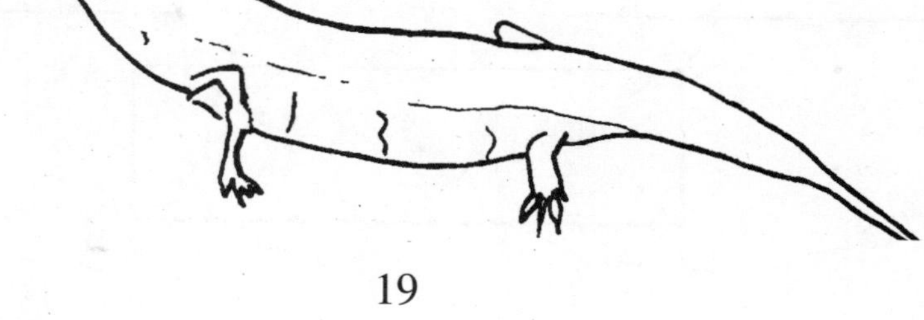

The संयोग Express

Help these trains link up together. Read the sounds on each carriage and then write them together as a full word.

....

....

....

....

....

Reading Practice

Read the following:

पुष्पम्
आस्यम्
आत्मा
कृष्णः
हस्तः
पश्यति
शम्भुः
प्लवनम्
मत्स्यः
अस्ति

Story 1: The Man and Krishna

Read and copy the following:

1. एकः नरः अस्ति।

2. नरः शम्भुः नाम।

3. शम्भुः वनम् नगरात् गच्छति।

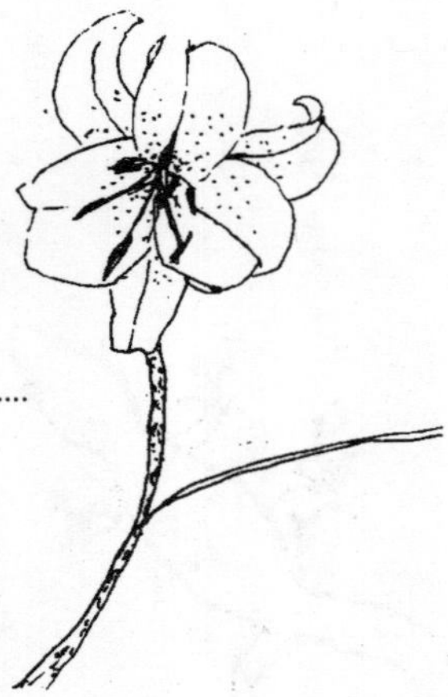

4. वने शम्भुः कृष्णम् पश्यति।

5. शम्भुः वदति हे कृष्ण इति।

6. शम्भुः पुष्पम् कृष्णाय ददाति।

Note to Teacher/Student: As the students gain confidence, reading of the संयोग *examples can become faster.*
For instance, the first example can be read as 'ष्, ठ इति ष्ठ'.

Double - Decker संयोग

Sometimes the second letter goes underneath the first.

Read and copy these:

ष् + ठ → ष्ठ ....

द् + ध → द्ध ....

द् + व → द्व ....

क् + क → क्क ....

ङ् + ग → ङ्ग ....

Now join these:

द् + ध → ....

द् + व → ....

क् + क → ....

ष् + ठ → ....

ङ् + ग → ....

In the space below, draw your own double-decker bus driving through the jungle!

The Bus

Help the bus make the right stops!

Reading Practice

Read the following across:

त	ति	तिष्	तिष्ठ
श	शु	शुद्	शुद्ध
द्व	द्वा	द्वार	द्वारम्
कु	कुक्	कुक्कु	कुक्कुरः
अ	अङ्	अङ्ग	अङ्गः

Reading Practice

Read the following and then copy:

कुक्कुरः	
शुद्ध	
द्वारम्	
गच्छति	
तिष्ठ	
पश्यति	
अङ्गः	
जङ्गलः	

The Monkey Game

DANGER! Some of the words you have read have come apart. The pieces are scattered on the page. Help the monkeys fix them by drawing a vine between the two parts of the word. The first one is done for you.

तिष्	कुरः
द्वा	गः
शुद्	यति
कुक्	ठ
अङ्	गलः
पश्	ध
गच्	रम्
जङ्	छति

Story 2:
The Dog and the Two Sages

Read and copy the following:

1. एकः कुक्कुरः अस्ति।

....

2. कुक्कुरः नारङ्गः नाम।

....

3. नारङ्गः जङ्गले वसति।

....

4. द्वौ शुद्धौ ऋषी जङ्गलम् आगच्छतः।

....

....

5. कुक्कुरः वदति हे ऋषी उपविशतम्
इति।

6. ऋषी पीठयोः उपविशतः।

7. कुक्कुरः तु तिष्ठति॥

Daily Reading Chart 13

The Racing Track

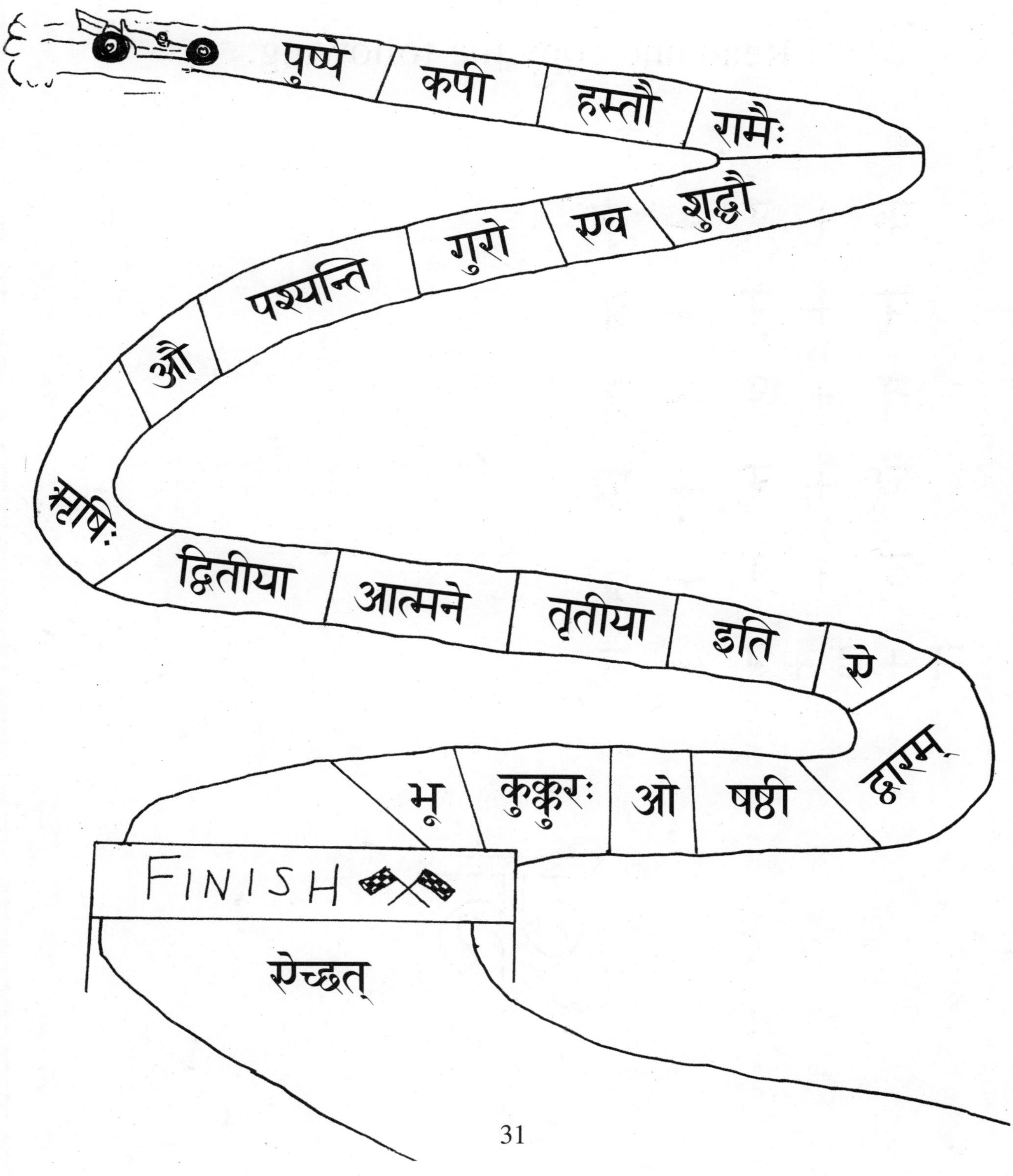

The Leg

When the sound र comes second in a संयोग
we write it like a leg that sticks out.

Read and copy the following:

क् + र → क्र

प् + र → प्र

त् + र → त्र

घ् + र → घ्र

द् + र → द्र

न् + द् + र → न्द्र

Now join these:

द् + र → ....

क् + र → ....

त् + र → ....

प् + र → ....

घ् + र → ....

न् + द् + र → ....

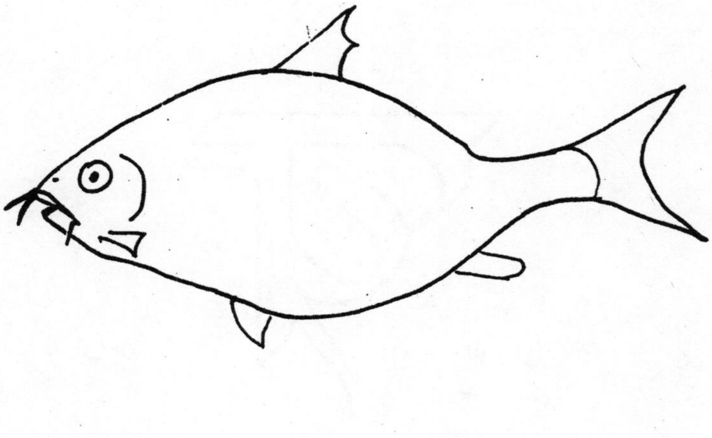

Read the following:

द्र न्द्र	क्र क्रि
प्र प्रब	त्र यत्र

घ्र घ्रम्

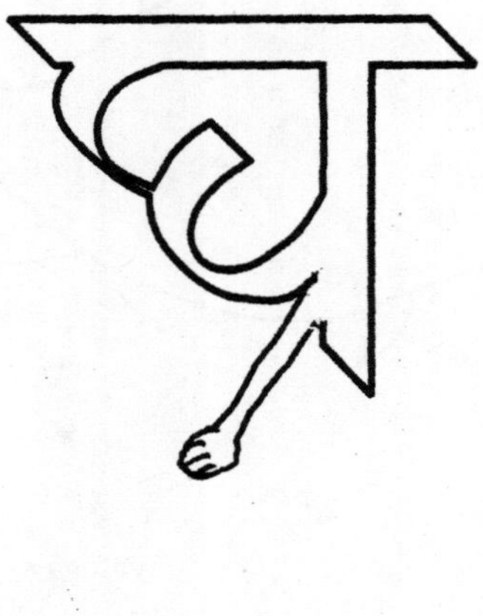

Reading Practice

Read the following across:

च	चन्	चन्द्	चन्द्रः
क	क्र	क्रि	क्रिया
प	प्र	प्रब	प्रबलः
शी	शीघ्	शीघ्र	शीघ्रम्
य	यत्	यत्र	यत्र यत्र

Reading Practice

Read the following and then copy:

यत्र यत्र	
तत्र तत्र	
शीघ्रम्	
प्रबलः	
क्रिया	
चन्द्रः	

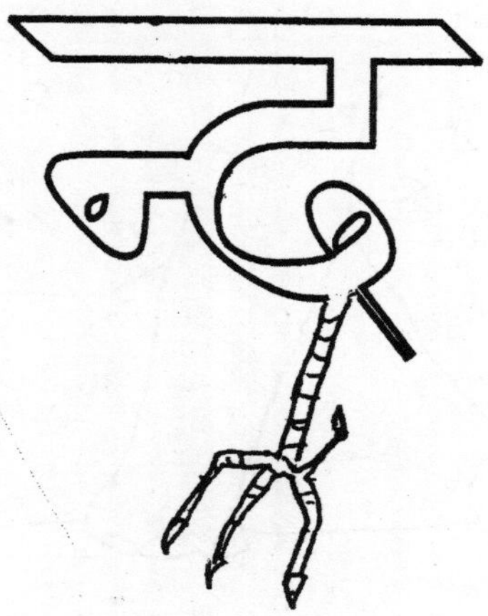

The Famous र Fishing-Hook

When a र comes first in a संयोग
then it is replaced by a hook above the top line.

Read and copy the following:

र् + ग → र्ग ....

र् + ण → र्ण ....

र् + ज → र्ज ....

र् + प → र्प ....

र् + य → र्य ....

र् + घ → र्घ ....

र् + व → र्व ....

Now join these:

र् + घ → ....

र् + ग → ....

र् + व → ....

र् + ण → ....

र् + य → ....

र् + प → ....

र् + ज → ....

Reading and Writing Practice

Read the following across, then copy:

मा	मार्	मार्ग	मार्गः
....	....	....	....
व	वर्	वर्ण	वर्णः
....	....	....	....
स	सर्	सर्प	सर्पः
....	....	....	....

[more on next page]

[continued]

सू   सूर्   सूर्य   सूर्यः

दी   दीर्   दीर्घ   दीर्घः

स   सर्   सर्व   सर्वम्

अर्   अर्ज   अर्जु   अर्जुनः

Reading Practice

Read the following:

सर्वम्
दीर्घः
सूर्यः
सर्पः
अर्जुनः
वर्णः
मार्गः

Where Do We Put the Fishing-Hook?

So far we have put the र् hook above the final line of each letter.

Look where it comes in these:

र्ण   र्प   र्ग

Now see where the र् hook goes when the letter is followed by आ, ई, ओ and औ.

र्णा	र्णी	र्णो	र्णौ
र्पा	र्पी	र्पो	र्पौ
र्गा	र्गी	र्गो	र्गौ

Now read these!

The Fishing Game

Help the fisherman catch the fish by reading them.

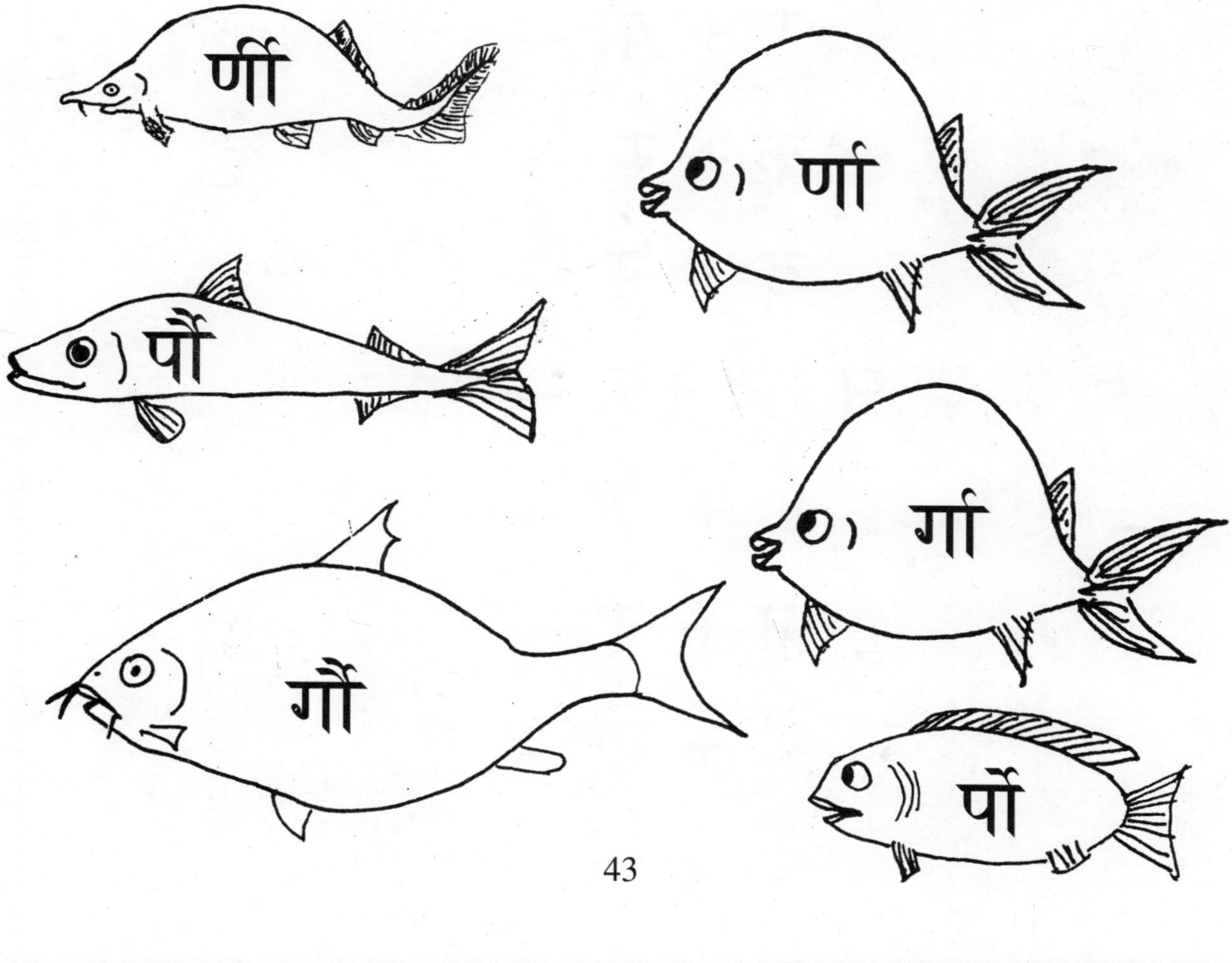

Revision of र संयोग

Join the following, then read aloud:

त् + र → ....

प् + र → ....

र् + प → ....

र् + घ → ....

र् + घा → ....

घ् + र → ....

र् + वी → ....

क् + र → ....

द् + र → ....

न् + द् + र → ....

र् + ज → ....

ग् + र → ....

र् + यो → ....

Story 3:
Kṛṣṇa's Mother, Yaśodā, Sees All Things in His Mouth

Read and copy the following:

1. यशोदा कृष्णम् गच्छति।

2. कृष्णः हसति।

3. यशोदा तस्य आस्यम् पश्यति।

4. तत्र यशोदा सूर्यम् पश्यति।

5. तत्र यशोदा चन्द्रम् पश्यति।

[more on next page]

[continued]

6. तत्र यशोदा वनम् पश्यति।

7. तत्र यशोदा सर्वम् पश्यति।

Now you can draw a picture of Yaśodā looking into Kṛṣṇa's mouth! What does she see there ?

Daily Reading Chart 14

LEGS AND HOOKS

प्रबलः
सर्पः
क्रिया
सूर्ये
तत्र
चन्द्रः
मार्गः
सर्व
वर्णः
प्रेम

Special संयोग

Read the following, then copy
the संयोग three times.

त् + त → त्त   त्त

ज् + ञ → ज्ञ   ज्ञ

श् + र → श्र   श्र

ह् + र → ह्र   ह्र

क् + त → क्त   क्त

क् + ष → क्ष   क्ष

Practise क्ष a few more times:

क्ष   क्ष   क्ष   क्ष

Now try क्ष on your own!

Now join these:

क् + ष →

ह् + र →

ज् + ञ →

क् + त →

श् + र →

त् + त →

Now read the following:

त	त्ता
क्ष	क्षः
क्त	क्ति
ज्ञ	ज्ञा
श्र	श्री
ह्र	ह्रस्

Reading Practice

Read the following across, then copy:

श्र	श्री	
स	सत्त	सत्ता
व	वृ	वृक्षः
ज्ञा	ज्ञान	ज्ञानम्
मु	मुक्त	मुक्तिः

Reading Practice

Read the following across, then copy:

श्रीः	....
सत्ता	....
वृक्षः	....
मुक्तिः	....
ज्ञानम्	....
अक्षरम्	....

Story 4: The Snake-Demon and the Pure Man

Read and copy the following:

1. एकः सर्पः अस्ति।

2. सर्पः राक्षसः अस्ति।

3. राक्षसः वृक्षे वसति।

4. शुद्धः नरः राक्षसस्य वृक्षम् गच्छति।

5. नरः वदति गच्छ हे राक्षस इति।

6. राक्षसः वदति अहो अहो इति।

7. राक्षसः वृक्षात् प्लवनम् करोति।

8. राक्षसः वृक्षात् धावति।

9. नरः गृहम् गच्छति॥

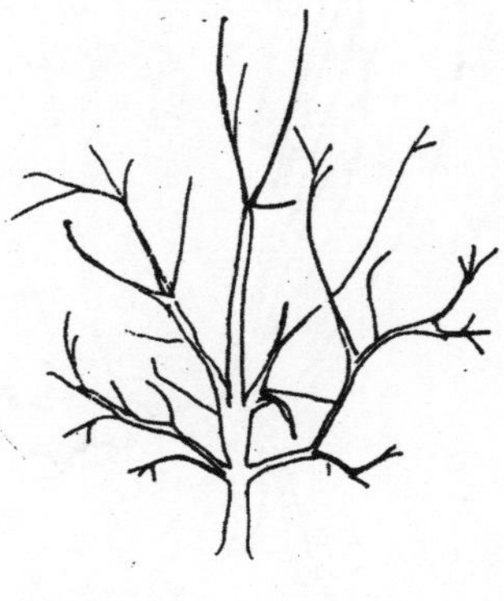

Champion Reader's Prize

If your reading is excellent, play this game. Write your favourite letters or words in the balloons. Then colour them in.

The Great Animal Quiz

See how many letters and words you can read.

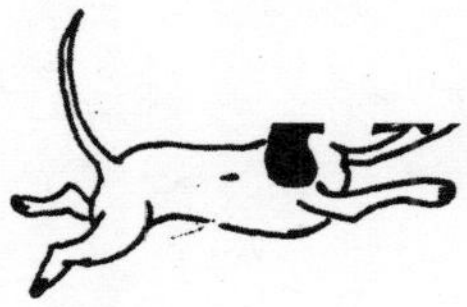

अ इ उ ए ओ औ

क गा मि सी बु लृ दे

को हृ पृ तै नौ

नरः रथः गजः खगः नारी

नृपः तम् विश् यजुस्

पश्य शुद्धः द्वारम्

Preparation for the Final Story

Fill in these संयोग and then read them.

ह् + र → ....

स् + व → ....

ध् + न → ....

Now read and copy the following:

ह ह्र ह्रस् ह्रस्वः

....

ब बध् बध्न बध्ना बध्नाति

....

Story 5: Yaśodā Cannot Bind the Limitless Kṛṣṇa

Read and copy the following final story:

1. कृष्णः नवनीतम् हस्तेन खादति।

   ....

2. यशोदा कृष्णम् गच्छति।

   ....

3. कृष्णः धावति।

   ....

4. यशोदा कृष्णम् सूत्रेण बध्नाति।

   ....

[more on next page]

[continued]

5. सूत्रम् ह्रस्वम् अस्ति।

6. द्वितीयेन सूत्रेण यशोदा कृष्णम् बध्नाति।

7. द्वितीयम् सूत्रम् ह्रस्वम् अस्ति।

8. तृतीयेन सूत्रेण यशोदा कृष्णम् बध्नाति।

[continued]

9. तृतीयम् सूत्रम् ह्रस्वम् पुनः अस्ति।

....

....

10. कृष्णः अनन्तः।

....